Where's Gramma?

Tricia Gardella and Greg David

STRING IS THE MOST IMPORTANT INVENTION EVER!

Published by Write 'em Cowgirl Publishing
To contact the author, write to the publisher at:
trigar@mlode.com

Copyright © Tricia Gardella
Write 'em Cowgirl Publishing 2023

WRITE 'EM COWGIRL PUBLISHING

Where's Gramma?
by Tricia Gardella
Illustrated by Greg David

Category:
JUVENILE FICTION / Family
Paperback ISBN: 978-1-959412-19-9
Hardback ISBN: 978-1-959412-20-5
Library of Congress Control Number: 2023938664

Edited and designed by
Emerald Books
emerald-books.com

Synopsis:
The grandchildren think they know everything about Gramma. But Gramma isn't always as predictable as they think. Finding Gramma turns out to be a wild adventure!

Where's Gramma ?

Up in the tree.

Where's Gramma ?

DIGGING A TRENCH.

WATER, THEN CONCRETE.

Voilà, a new bench.

Where's Gramma?

Down by
the lake.

Where's Gramma?

COLLECTING SOME BUGS.

BEETLES. GRASSHOPPERS.
BUTTERFLIES. SLUGS.

STUDYING A HOLE.

"LOOK HERE, JACK.
IT'S THE HOME OF A MOLE."

Where's Gramma?

SWIMMING THE POOL.

A JACKKNIFE.
A CANNONBALL.
OH, HOW COOL.

Where's Gramma?

OUT IN THE PEN.

Where's Gramma?

MILKING THE COW.

Where's Gramma?

CHOOSING A BOOK.

"COME HERE, BOYS,
COME TAKE A LOOK."

Where's Gramma?

KNITTING A HAT, SWEATER,
OR MITTENS. STUFF LIKE THAT.

The End

About the Author

Tricia Gardella's books are mostly influenced by the ranch life she stepped into sixty years ago. She writes children's books about ranch animals, ranch routines, and ranch relationships, though she occasionally gets side-tracked to explore the myriad other sides of life. She has tried it all, and almost mastered some: canning, cooking, knitting and other fiber arts, rug-making, gardening, and various business ventures. But writing is her happiest of places and she is thrilled to be back after a twenty-year sabbatical. She has a BA in Ancient History and Classical Archaeology, three children, seven grandchildren, and three great grandchildren, all giving her much food for thought. She lives with two self-centered cats in Central California.

About the Illustrator

Greg David is a children's book illustrator hailing from the beautiful country of Wales. With a passion for creating captivating illustrations that bring stories to life, his aim is to leave a lasting impression on young readers worldwide through his distinct visual that is both whimsical and vibrant. Greg's illustrations have graced the pages of numerous children's books, offering young readers a visual gateway into the captivating worlds created by talented storytellers. For more information, visit www.cartoonboy.co.uk

More great books from Tricia Gardella

WRITE 'EM COWGIRL PUBLISHING

Grandma's Kitchen

by Tricia Gardella
Illustrated by
Karen Donnelly

Sssssspt!

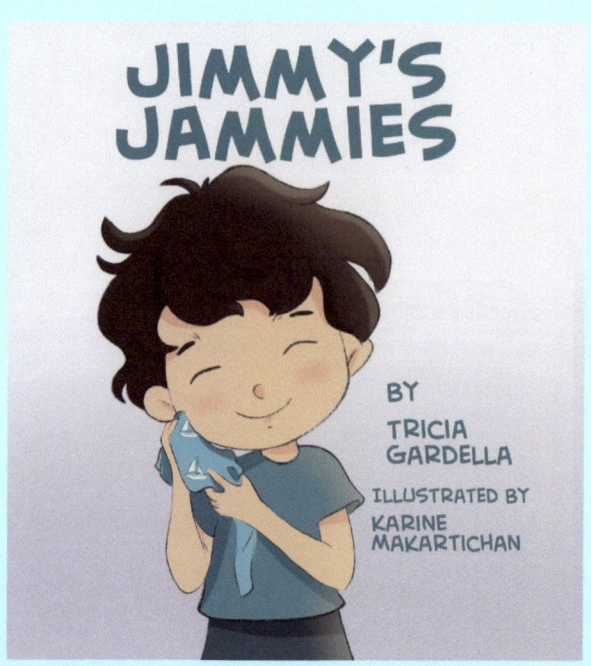

JIMMY'S JAMMIES

BY
TRICIA
GARDELLA

ILLUSTRATED BY
KARINE
MAKARTICHAN

GRAMPA JACK PUT IT BACK

BY TRICIA GARDELLA
ILLUSTRATED BY
RACHEL BAINES

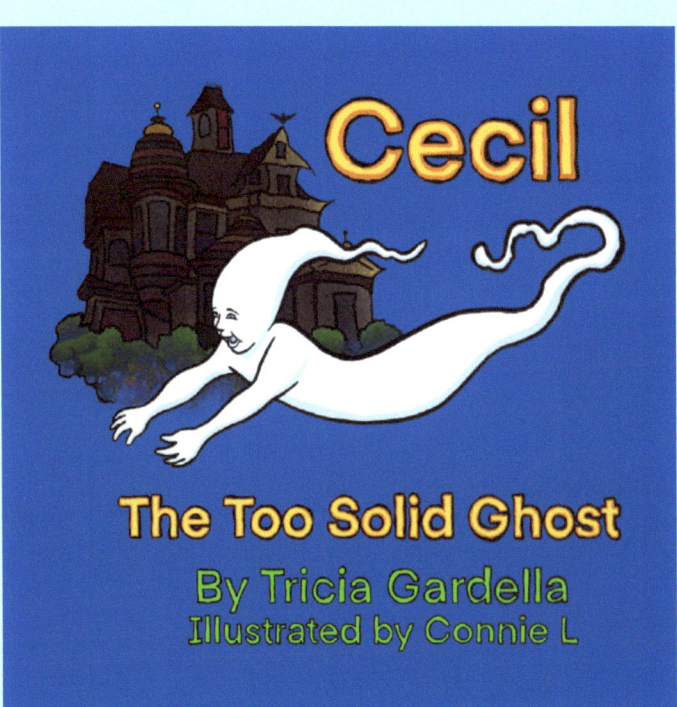

Cecil

The Too Solid Ghost

By Tricia Gardella
Illustrated by Connie L

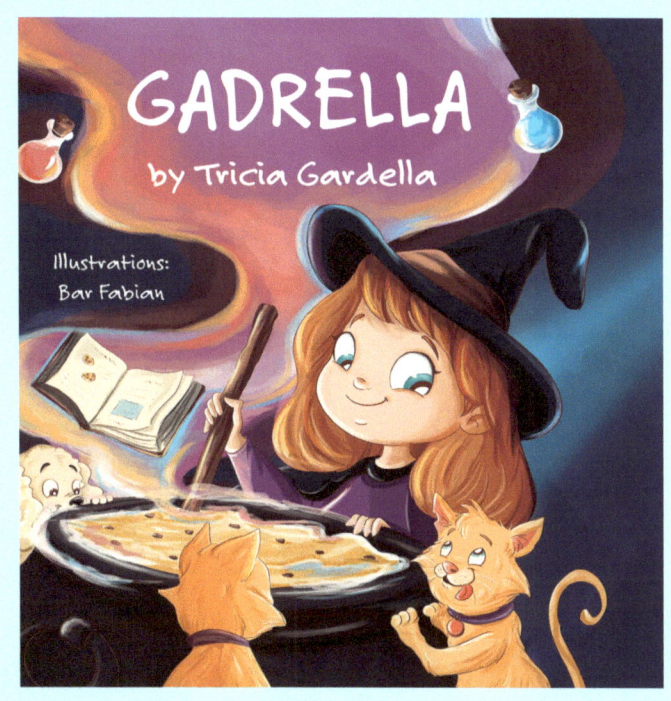

GADRELLA

by Tricia Gardella

Illustrations:
Bar Fabian

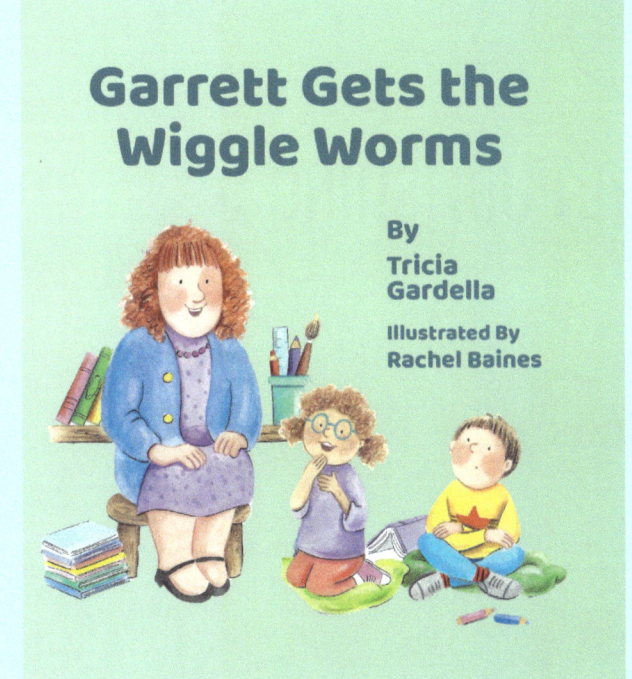

Garrett Gets the Wiggle Worms

By
Tricia
Gardella

Illustrated By
Rachel Baines

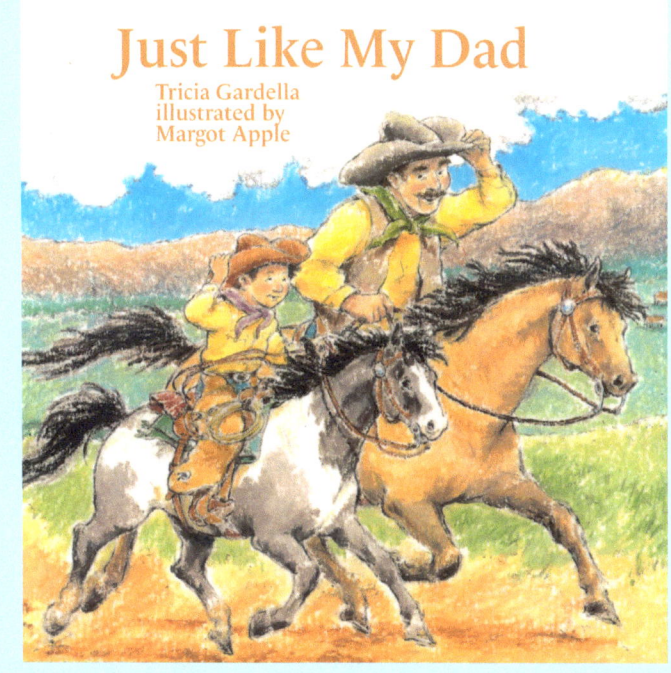

Just Like My Dad

Tricia Gardella
illustrated by
Margot Apple

IF YOU LIKED THIS BOOK, PLEASE TAKE A MOMENT TO REVIEW IT ON AMAZON!

WRITE 'EM COWGIRL PUBLISHING

triciagardella.com